j 808.042
Hug

Hughes, Riley

How to write creatively.

How to Write Creatively

BY RILEY HUGHES

A Language Skills Concise Guide
FRANKLIN WATTS
New York | London | Toronto | Sydney | 1980

This book is for
Walter and Shirley

Library of Congress Cataloging in Publication Data

Hughes, Riley.
How to write creatively.

(A Language skills concise guide)
Includes index.
1. Creative writing (Secondary education)—
Juvenile literature. I. Title. II. Series:
Language skills concise guide.
LB1631.H83   808'.042   80–15689
ISBN 0–531–04128–X

Contents

How to Write Creatively

Chapter 1.
Your Creative
Source

We live at one and the same time in the world we see and the world we imagine. Both worlds are ours to claim, and they fit well together. All around us is an "out there" for us to move around in and explore. This is the world we "see." How we grasp what strikes our minds, how we interpret what comes to us through the senses, how we find meaning—that is what we "imagine."

To imagine is to create. Creation expands, fulfills, draws out significances. The way to create, of course, is to recreate. We reassemble that enormous world outside of us and make it, through our thoughts and our emotions, an expression of ourselves.

Some of what we "see" we remember. We store all sorts of impressions. They come back to us in one of two basic ways. They return without effort or even control while we dream, awake or asleep. They also come on demand. We search in our imagination for an appropriate image, or perhaps we form a new image by combining several that were there before.

What we remember and use, we use by means of language.

Our first creative use of language occurs in early childhood. We begin making the world ours when we attach names to objects. Nouns come first. "Tree." "Ball." "Car." Already we are asserting the power of the writer. To write is, first of all, to give names to things. To be able to put a name to something is, for a writer, to be able to control it.

Verbs come next. We imitate then describe actions; we make demands. After a time, pronouns appear in our speech. When they do, it is a sign that imagination is at work in our life. Imagination has taken a huge stride forward when our world comes to include both "bird" and "me."

Our most admired writers frequently display in their work the fresh-eyed candor of a child. Natural or practiced, this quality of openness can be of immense value to a writer. To the young the world is a vivid place. Each object in it is a thing of wonder. To the creative person at any age, what is seen and experienced, even many times over, can never become trite or stale. Firsthand experience—like tomorrow morning—is forever sparkling and new.

Words can make life so. Words have the power to capture and preserve the freshness of things. They can cause any object to be present to the mind when the object itself is absent, when it lives only in memory. Creativeness recreates and gives permanence to what is gone and can never come back.

In music, sculpture, painting, or writing, creativity "fixes." It takes possession of a passing moment, event, thought, or feeling. Whatever it captures, it gives form to. A painter's thought takes the form of a color or a shape; a poet's thought becomes a line of verse.

Creativity aims at expressing the exactness of whatever is recalled, at the precise emotion, whether of joy or sadness, originally present. Each art has its own proper medium by means of which it seizes the fleeting moment. In writing, the means is a net of words.

Words function best when they do not call undue attention to themselves. They are most exact when they do not seem to be language. Words that fit have a kind of invisibility about them. They do not appear to be labels attached to things; rather, they are the skin of the things themselves.

Words succeed in their mission when parts of speech become expressions of reality. To express reality so that every word is clear and natural, with the proper words in the proper places, should be the goal of all who write.

Expressing reality through words is often an elusive matter, and its pursuit can become a lifelong struggle. The ability to write creatively is both a birthright and something that must be fought for over and over—and each time achieved with difficulty.

It is not enough to merely watch what is going on around us. Creativity is not passive; it is awareness not only *of* action but *in* action. "None of them knew the color of the sky," begins Stephen Crane's famous short story of shipwrecked men in an open boat. To be creative means to be constantly alert to the nature of whatever sea or sky surrounds us. "Be one of those people," Henry James advises us, "upon whom nothing is lost."

We must, then, always be ready to communicate our experience. To be truly creative is to be aware of the opinions and feelings of others to the same degree that we are aware of our own. Long ago the French philosopher René Descartes gave us a formula for proving existence: "I think, therefore I am." Writing thus confirms in us the fact of our existence, since it is a response to the "out there," the other. I see, I respond, I create, I share; therefore I and the other both exist. Or, as Henry James, perhaps America's greatest novelist, liked to put it, "I OBSERVE . . . I VIBRATE!"

Our alertness must be expressed to be truly creative. Keeping everything bottled up inside is not the way to demonstrate creativity. When we respond creatively to stimuli—by gesture or word, spoken or written—communication happens. Only then is the circle complete.

Creativity includes rather than excludes. When Katherine Anne Porter was asked if she were a particular character in her novel *Ship of Fools,* she replied, "Yes, I am that woman. I am also the Spanish dancers. I am the bulldog. I am the ship. I am the ocean."

Creativity, especially in writing, starts with inner awareness. But the finish line is in sharing.

Inspiration has a significant part to play in the process of creating. Yet inspiration—a kind of dictation from something inside us, our subconscious perhaps—comes seldom enough, and then it gives us only part of what we need to produce. It is like suddenly seeing where two or three jigsaw puzzle pieces fit, but then having to work hours to complete the puzzle. Similarly, we must work at giving full-bodied form to inspiration.

The poet A. E. Housman tells of having whole stanzas of a poem flash into his mind one day while he was standing on a street corner waiting to cross. What came to him without any conscious effort on his part was a poem—an unfinished poem. Yet it took him six months to write the last two stanzas of that poem.

Housman's efforts clearly illustrate the two-stage process of creative writing. In the first stage, the poet's mind must be open to the images and ideas that flood it. In the second stage, the writer must be equally creative. He or she must possess the discipline to hammer out, word by word, line by line, what did not come freely by inspiration.

Inspiration, of course, does not always follow the sequence it did with Housman. Sometimes inspiration plunges into the middle of a creative effort. At other times, all the necessary parts may be present, but not in order; then suddenly, the writer is able to arrange the parts so that the whole comes alive.

To be creative is, first of all, to be open to any gift that comes to mind unbidden—any idea or image with generating power.

"Sunday passed," wrote a student, "like an elderly woman crossing the road." Unless this is automatic writing, these words came from somewhere in the writer's mind. Had the writer once observed an elderly woman slowly making her way across a quiet street? Did the writer happen to be looking out the window on a gloomy Sunday seeing nothing in particular when the memory of that woman struck him? Or had the writer tried comparison after comparison in an abstract way before arriving at the image of the elderly woman to represent a boring Sunday passing slowly?

No matter. As Louis Pasteur said, "Chance favors the prepared mind." In each of these instances—Housman's poem and the student's paper—the process must be called creative. To work out a whole from a mere hint, interlocking word with word, is also creative. It is a matter of seeing first, then supplying a focus.

To begin with, look around you and observe. Record everything in your mind. Know, for example, what a wooden fence looks like after a rain shower, how snow sits on fenceposts, what bends in wind and biting rain. Find words to "film" what you see. Be dissatisfied with a sunset until you can describe its exact colors in a sentence.

Do you remember the child's game of placing your hand on paper and then tracing it? Place your hand on paper in another way—in words that give an accurate picture of its fleshiness. Describe the shape of your fingers and the way your thumb projects. How does your hand look in moments of tension? How does it look in moments of repose?

Sight is the sense we use the most. But it is not the only sense a writer exercises or attempts to capture in words. A creative person will be aware of things *seen* (three leafless trees against the sky); things *felt* (the coarse, aging bark of an oak tree trunk, a piece of silk drawn through the fingers); things *heard* (sirens, a baby's thin cry, two dogs in the distance); and things *tasted* (a pickle, a seeded bun, a lump of sugar, a lemon, an avocado). Be aware of all objects that affect the senses, and find words for the sensations they cause in you.

Know, then, what comes to you through your senses.

Know it, possess it, express it in words. To be truly creative is to know. It is to be able to grasp and record things with the accuracy of a photograph. It is also to be able to comprehend below-surface meaning with the insight of a painting.

Chapter 2.
Back to
Basics

The basic fact about writing is that it is written. It does not appear by itself. Somebody has to write it.

Writing is presented to us in so many hundreds of ways and so continuously that we have come to take it for granted, as if it were a fact of nature, like a leaf, a stone, or a cloud.

During communication, a message—a thought, an opinion, a request—is coming from someone and going to someone else. Communication is the process of sending and receiving.

The means of communication is the sentence, either implied, as in "Expir. date Sept. 23, 1981" or "ROW B SEAT 7," or completed, as in "This certificate is not transferable."

The implied sentence has limited use. It is often inadequate to communicate feeling, for example. It cannot make us laugh or cry. It cannot entertain. But the complete sentence can convey an emotion, a scientific law, or a principle. It can bring history or fiction to life.

Writing is words, but clearly it is more than words. With

words you have only begun to communicate. You need sentences to complete your thought.

Each sentence expresses one complete thought. It does this through a subject-verb-object relationship. A word group that does not form a sentence does not communicate.

The normal order of the English sentence is subject, verb, object: *I like apples.* For emphasis, this order may be inverted: *Apples I like!* But the same idea is not communicated when the same words are set down at random: *Like apples I.*

Punctuation can be as essential to the meaning of a sentence as word order. Written punctuation is the signal for the eye to break up the succession of words it sees into meaningful units.

Speed in sending and receiving is an essential factor in communication. Punctuation provides speed. It also allows for degrees of difficulty in what is being said. The more difficult the thought, the greater the need for punctuation to help make that thought clear.

Punctuation can be overused as well as underused. The dash and the terminal exclamation point, for example, should be used only sparingly, for best effect. The dash is properly used whenever there is a sudden shift in thought. Too many dashes announce a loss of control.

Note punctuation marks in your reading. See if you can tell how they are being used. They should be helping you to receive the message with greater ease and clarity. That is their purpose.

Commas and semicolons and the other marks of punctuation have their uses, but mechanics should never substitute for words. Mechanical devices serve to make the relationships between words clear—to indicate where the eye should pause, where it should stop.

Punctuation, as we have been saying, is a signal to the eye. So is paragraph indentation. New paragraphs are the strongest kind of punctuation. They convey the message that the writer will now pursue a different thought or topic.

Paragraphing, whether for fiction or nonfiction, should be practiced constantly. Because paragraphs are the building blocks of communication—just as sentences are the irreducible units—too much care cannot be given to them. One way to become proficient in paragraphing is to try writing a seven-sentence paragraph every now and then, or to practice writing paragraphs two sentences longer than those you usually write. Your writing will improve for having made the task more difficult.

Like correct punctuation, correct spelling is a fundamental tool of writing, one often neglected and seldom given the consideration it deserves. Competence in spelling is a reasonable goal for every writer.

Yet it is unreasonable to expect from yourself perfection in this area. After all, one constantly hears new words, words pronounced but not spelled out. You should know enough, however, to be able to find nearly any word in the dictionary. You should also know by heart the spelling of the words you use frequently. And finally you should constantly be adding to your vocabulary of frequently used words.

Knowing spelling rules is helpful, but because the English vocabulary—the largest in the Indo-European language family—consists of words from many languages, there are many exceptions to the rules. Further, rules must be remembered and applied in their entirety to be of use. The "i before e" rule is dangerous to know unless you also know the second half of that rule, "except after c." And even that is not the whole rule.

Acquaint yourself with the rules, then. But also work at forming exact mental pictures of words, particularly the ones ending in *able* or *ible.*

Spelling is a matter of both ear-mindedness and eye-mindedness. You must hear a word correctly, master its syllabification, and then learn to both speak and write it correctly.

Type out or print in longhand a list of ten words that give you great difficulty, words you misspell every time you use them. Put your list up in a place where you will see it often. Three candidates for your list might well be *loneliness, commitment,* and *separate.* (Misspellers tend to leave out the "e" in the first and put two "t's" in the second; in the third, the second vowel is "a," not "e.")

Each day, visually "photograph" your list. When you are confident that you can spell some of the words on the list, remove those words and substitute others. Add words that are new to you, words that you have just heard or seen. You will be adding to your vocabulary as well as gaining confidence in spelling. And vocabulary, after all, is your primary resource if you hope to write.

Your attention to spelling and vocabulary will serve to remind you that you have three vocabularies at your command, not one only. You have three channels to word power: a speaking vocabulary, a reading vocabulary, and a writing vocabulary. The three overlap, of course; they also interact.

You acquired your speaking vocabulary first, and it is the one you use every day. Your reading vocabulary came next; it too should be exercised daily. Your reading vocabulary will grow in proportion to the amount, and to some extent the quality, of the reading you do.

Your writing vocabulary will, quite obviously, depend upon your two other vocabularies, upon the care and precision with which you speak, and upon the scope and quality of what you read.

Your goal is not to "talk like a book," nor to become slavishly dependent on books for what you think. It is to familiarize yourself with your language so that using it will be as easy and natural to you as breathing.

Chapter 3.
Writing Is
Thinking

To write is to think.

Expressing—pressing out—our thoughts in words is a little like having "second thoughts." They are not very different from the words we used when first we put our thoughts or images together. Yet neither are they identical with the thinking we did the first time around.

Sometimes you hear people say, with more than a touch of smugness, "I'm not a writer," or "Not me, I can't write." Many people seem to think that writing is a specialty, like dentistry or computer programming. Yet you never hear anyone boast, "I'm no thinker. I can't think." Everyone recognizes that the right to think is a birthright, not a privilege to be extended to philosophers only. Most of us do not want others to do our thinking for us.

Just as we should want to grow in our ability to think for ourselves, so we should be determined to grow in our ability to express our thoughts in words, and this ability can best be developed by writing.

The ease with which words and ideas sometimes occur

to us may often disguise the relationship between thinking and writing. Entire sentences (perhaps needing some attention to their grammar) may spring to mind seemingly without effort on our part. We may find, however, that these words are inadequate to express what we really want to say. "How do I know what I think until I see what I say?" the poet W. H. Auden cautiously observed.

Written communication is always the result of thought. Even the most random, the most seemingly effortless, arrival of words in the mind has been prepared for. Words that are not already in our vocabulary simply cannot occur to us. We inherit language from our culture; we do not invent it for ourselves.

Literary thought, like all thought, begins with the knowledge and the use of words. Single words and words in combination are the tools of literary thinking. To think and to write creatively we must learn to use these tools.

Examine the following sentences, each made vivid by a single word.

1. The sun shone indifferently down on them.
2. She was voracious for a kind word and a smile.
3. She wiped the crumbs from a tidy mouth.
4. He faded slowly into the winged armchair.
5. Her voice was low, with a catch in it, like a tide tripping in retreat over pebbles.
6. The corn shot up like statistics.
7. Nature, for enticement, gave Cape Cod a hook, confident of Pilgrims and tourists to come.
8. Dawn invaded their eyelids.
9. Thoughts of vengeance began to populate his mind.

The words that activate these sentences are the following: *indifferently, voracious, tidy, faded, tripping, statistics, confident, invaded,* and *populate.* Note in the fourth sentence the difference in suggested meaning between the expected "sank" and the verb actually used. The latter suggests some kind of indecision, some weakness in the person performing the action. "Sank" is neutral; it does not direct the reader to a specific attitude to take about the actor or the action.

The creative use of words does two things. First, it allows the reader to see the object or the action (the noun or the verb) in a particular context of meaning. The words not only say something, they mean something. Each word in a column of words in the dictionary says something, that is, has significance and is a symbol of something. But together these words do not mean anything, just as a heap of stones do not make a wall. Equally important, the structuring of words causes the reader to receive a specific shade of meaning and no other.

First to see, then to cause others to see exactly what the writer saw—that is the object of all writing.

To achieve this exactness, the writer must use the right word—not, as Mark Twain put it, "its first cousin."

"First cousin" words miss the target. They are inexact or shopworn, sometimes both. Sound writing avoids them.

Consider the following:

1.　It is thought to be a fine movie.
2.　The thing is, such things are dangerous.
3.　Needless to say, their friends cracked up.

Why are these three sentences slipshod? The first avoids responsibility. Writers should always be in control of their sentences, of their meaning. Who thought it? Thought what precisely? "Fine" is one of the most overworked words in spoken and written English. Avoid it.

In the second sentence the word "thing" (which can be applied to every object a noun can be used for) is to be avoided whenever possible. If used at all, it should be employed sparingly, certainly not twice within one sentence.

The third sentence contains the two greatest enemies of originality in thought and expression: the cliché and slang. "Needless to say" (or its twin, "It goes without saying") is perhaps the most mindless word group ever coined.

Both these witless phrases contain a built-in contradiction. Both amount to saying, "You know already what I am going to say, but I am going to bore you with it anyway."

You will know a cliché by the numbness it brings on; it is a prepacked word group. Whenever words come to you in clusters and have a familiar ring, you undoubtedly are remembering a cliché.

The use of slang is another way of impeding communication and warding off creativity. "Cracked up" will be recognized as slang, and out-of-date slang at that. Slang withers quickly; it hides meaning from all but a few. If you admit slang words and expressions into your thinking, you will have limited your capacity to create, and you will be communicating exclusively with those who understand the slang and are willing to forgive you for it. Those who don't understand will try to discover a literal meaning in what you write—but they won't find one.

Slang is the opposite of literal; it is figurative—a kind of misplaced poetry pretending to be prose. "When the dishes fell from the sink, they cracked up." Now that is literal. It means exactly what it says. Therefore, it is not slang.

In a sense, of course, slang is creative. It can catch the tone or color of the moment, and when first seen or heard, it bears all the appearance of freshness. But this freshness soon wears off. New moments bring new slang with them. You will notice that slang constantly replaces itself—new words and new word groups appear, saying the same thing. The earlier slang has disappeared, no longer being acceptable.

Sometimes slang is a kind of secret code; it is the intention of such slang to conceal meaning from all but a few. (An extreme example would be the slang, or argot, of criminals.) This slang, far from being sprightly and attractive, is the bad manners of language, or the language of bad manners.

It should be noted that we are speaking here of the use of slang in nonfiction only. If you are writing fiction, with characters who would normally use slang, it would be absurd to correct their language for them. Under those circumstances, slang is not only allowable, it is necessary.

In neither fiction nor nonfiction is the correct choice of words always easy to make. Words reflect reality, and reality can be downright awkward at times. Take these three ways of expressing the same reality:

> illegal alien
> wetback
> undocumented person

There is something cold and repelling about the first. The second is cruel and insulting. As for the third, it is evasive, unwilling to pass judgment. Without using any of these terms, try to express, in a sentence or two, the social reality of the matter—first in general, abstract terms, then in highly personal ones, perhaps describing a particular family.

Words have two kinds of reality about them: denotative and connotative. They "de-note" when they define; they "con-note" when they suggest.

Using words creatively means knowing their derivation —their root sense—as well as their current connotative sense. When a word may be taken in more than one sense, place the word in a context that cannot fail to make clear to the reader the sense you mean.

Knowing the spirit of your time does not mean that you —or the words you use—must meekly conform to it. A great writer once said that the spirit of creativity is the spirit of contradiction. Suppose you find yourself in opposition to the accepted beliefs of your time. Seek out words that will express your point of view, your slant on things. The creative spirit is essentially that of the boy in the fairy tale who blurted out before everyone, "But the emperor *has* no clothes."

The more you experience, the more you observe, the more you will be aware of the *two*-ness of most things. We move in a duality of time (then/now) and of space (here/

there). Change is the law of life. Change is constant, the only constancy we can count on.

The concept of change provides us with a basic creative writing device, the device of contrast. With this device we can build verbal structures ranging in size and substance from a compound sentence to a full-length book. Dickens in *A Tale of Two Cities* begins: "It was the best of times, it was the worst of times . . . it was the spring of hope, it was the winter of despair, we had everything before us, we had nothing before us. . . ."

In his "Sonnet 65" Shakespeare makes powerful use of the device of contrast to portray change. Note, even if you have to read it three times, what happens in the sonnet's opening movement, as the poet pursues his concept of time as destroyer:

> Since brass, nor stone, nor earth, nor boundless sea,
> But sad mortality o'er-sways their power,
> How with this rage shall beauty hold a plea,
> Whose action is no stronger than a flower?
> O, how shall summer's honey breath hold out
> Against the wreckful siege of battering days,
> When rocks impregnable are not so stout,
> Nor gates of steel so strong, but Time decays?

The following poems by two leading Victorian poets illustrate the literary capabilities of the device of contrast. Robert Browning's "Parting at Morning" uses imagery from nature to provide the contrast for something abstract, a resolution:

> Round the cape of a sudden came the sea,
> And the sun looked over the mountain's rim—
> And straight was a path of gold for him,
> And the need of a world of men for me.

The sun's way and the poet's need are contrasted; hence the implication of the title.

Alfred Lord Tennyson's "The Eagle" presents, with force

and vividness, not so much a thought as the representation of an action:

> He clasps the crag with crooked hands;
> Close to the sun in lonely lands,
> Ring'd with the azure world, he stands.
>
> The wrinkled sea beneath him crawls;
> He watches from his mountain walls,
> And like a thunderbolt he falls.

Did you note the contrast between the final word in Tennyson's first stanza and the final word in his second? Consider the contrasting verbs used to describe the motion of the sea and the movement of the eagle. In the first five lines the eagle, so to speak, posed for his photograph. In the sixth, he is on film.

The poems may be compared as well as contrasted. Both rely upon observation of nature. Yet herein lies a contrast. Tennyson's poem seems to remain entirely within the world of nature, whereas Browning's poem uses nature in order to express a preference for the "world of men." A further examination reveals still another comparison. Both poems use personification of nature: the sun "looked"; the eagle possesses "hands."

Poetry uses words more intensely than does prose, to symbolize, to suggest meanings, and to evoke emotions. Poetry is known for its sparseness, its economy of words. In its use of words, poetry gets the most out of the least.

In prose writing we can also find a good measure of intensity and an economic use of words, but the thinking is less constrained and not as concentrated.

To create either poetry or prose, thinking and feeling are essential. Feelings drive, thinking directs. Writing in any form depends upon both, but feelings remain formless without the thinking that puts them into words and sentences.

Now we are ready to examine in greater detail how reading thoroughly—and reading imaginatively—can help us to write creatively.

Chapter 4.
Reading for
Writing's Sake

"I never read much; I have something else to do," boasts John Thorpe, a boorish braggart in a Jane Austen novel. The author treats her character with amused disdain, particularly because of his scorn for novels, works he describes as "the stupidest things in creation."

No one who hopes for success in using language creatively can afford to imitate John Thorpe's dismissal of reading. To read nearly everything makes much more sense for the future writer than to read almost nothing. It is even better to read compulsively, everything from magazines and books to the information on a breakfast cereal package, than not to read at all.

Nothing is more decisive in forming a writer—or indeed in forming a creative person—than the habit of reading. Organized knowledge starts with exposure to the printed word. Reading, as Francis Bacon put it long ago, makes "a full man." The creative user of words never existed who was not a reader first.

There are many reasons why this is so. For one thing, creativity is not the same as originality. Originality in writing in the total sense is no longer attainable. Language and literature have already been invented. Before we come to use them, words already *mean.* We are the inheritors, not the formers, of language. The pioneering has already been done. We come in now at a stage when both our language and its literature have long been in use and there is already an enormous body of work to be absorbed and built upon.

Over the centuries an American idiom has formed. (An idiom is, essentially, the way a particular branch of a language evolves.) As Americans, we can now claim our own culture and idiom, our own way of seeing, hearing, and speaking. The only means of discovering this idiom—of developing an ear for the hum of language—is through constant, repeated exposure to it through reading. Purposeful reading is culture in the highest sense.

During the past two hundred years America has fashioned a literature, a way of seeing and saying, that has taken its place among the literatures of the world. In the writings of Benjamin Franklin, James Madison, Edgar Allan Poe, Nathaniel Hawthorne, Abraham Lincoln, Mark Twain, Henry Adams, Henry James, Emily Dickinson, O. Henry, F. Scott Fitzgerald, Ernest Hemingway, William Faulkner, Flannery O'Connor, and Walter Lippmann—to name just a few —we have found our special identity as a people. The works of these writers and of countless others provide an idiomatic word hoard for all of us to draw from.

The writings of earlier generations of Americans provide a national resource that, during the years of our growth and maturation, we should make our own. A person cannot mature creatively without a knowledge of the work of his or her culture's representative writers.

Through a deliberate yet not overly rigid approach, we should become familiar with America's classic writers. This would mean, at a minimum, reading Poe, for ingenuity; Hawthorne, for subtlety; Mark Twain, for the perspective only humor can bring; and perhaps Henry James, for elegance. (Elegance, out of fashion now, may, in the cyclical nature of things, soon return.)

True, none of these writers will provide us with a picture of contemporary life. That is not why we read them. The daily newspaper, the news magazine, the how-to manual or textbook—even the cereal package—will do that.

Literature brings us news from a timeless world. As one poet put it, "Literature is news that *stays* alive." The past and the present, literature reminds us, should not be thought of as modes of retreat from one another; they make up the whole.

The short stories of Poe, then, should as soon as possible become part of the furniture of our minds. Too much sophistication, too varied an experience in reading, or too many hours of television viewing may blunt their effectiveness, their impact of surprise and novelty. These stories should be read in the morning of one's life, not left until later. Still, there are some, "The Fall of the House of Usher" and "The Gold Bug" among them, that will stamp their authority on the mind, however late one discovers them.

Many pieces of Hawthorne's fiction—particularly stories such as "Young Goodman Brown," "The Birthmark," and "Roger Malvin's Burial"—will read as though they were written only yesterday rather than over a century ago. The conflicts between science and morality that Hawthorne explores in "The Birthmark," for example, are still with us today. Similarly, Melville's character Bartleby—the man who says "I prefer not to"—symbolizes society's alienated individual as effectively today as he did a century ago.

"We all come out of that book," Ernest Hemingway said of Mark Twain's *Huckleberry Finn.* Hemingway was referring to his own work and that of the writers of his generation. Exiles in Paris though they were—perhaps even because they were—writers of the "Lost Generation" found that this story of a boy on a raft contains, like an acorn, a mighty oak of meaning. To miss reading *The Adventures of Huckleberry Finn* would be a little like drawing a map of America and leaving out the Mississippi River.

Huckleberry Finn's adventures on his timeless river point up a basic aspect of our national character: America is a country of three or four vast regions (countries in themselves), each unique in geography, climate, and history. American literature is made up of the sound of many voices, not one voice alone. It is impossible, for example, for a poet like Robert Frost to function as a nature poet for the entire country; the snowy evening of his famous poem "Stopping by Woods on a Snowy Evening" is a New Hampshire evening, not an Arizona evening. Even the birds of New England are different from those of the Southwest.

As a consequence of America's great size and complex history, we possess a rich body and a long tradition of regional literature. A growing number of regional magazines help us to understand our varied character. Creative readers alert to their development as writers will form intimate links with the literature—from bus timetables and weekly newspapers to biographies and novels—of at least one American region.

Our national roots come from the land, sea, and air around us, but we have other, even deeper roots, those of the language itself. Our linguistic and, to a degree, political beginnings are an ocean away—in England. As Americans, whether our personal or cultural origins are African, Asian, or European, we are the heirs of England's history and, above all, its language. The Norman Conquest of England, although it occurred several centuries before the discovery of America, is a central fact in our own history. Why? Because the Normans packed language in their luggage when they left for England in 1066.

Thus we are not only the heirs of Mark Twain, we are the heirs of Shakespeare also. A hundred years after Columbus, when our land still lay largely uninhabited and unexplored, Shakespeare's poems and plays were furnishing many of the insights and images we use today. This greatest of writers in our language played so large a role in forming modern English that four centuries later we are still thinking his thoughts—and thinking them in his words. Almost every line in Shakespeare is electric with energy and meaning. (The very verb "to be" carries echoes of Hamlet.) It is no exaggeration to say that English cannot now be written, or even thought, without Shakespeare.

Other English poets, and novelists too, can stock a mind hopeful of creation. An imagination that has not fed on the novels of Sir Walter Scott, Thomas Hardy, William Makepeace Thackeray, and, most of all, Charles Dickens, cannot be complete. This is true of Jane Austen too, although Mark Twain declared that leaving Jane Austen out was a good way of beginning one's library.

The resources of English prose go beyond those found in the great poets and novelists. English essays, biographies, and historical chronicles are equally fertile in rhythms and cadences to exercise the mind. Anyone who attends to the words of Jonathan Swift, James Boswell, Edmund Burke, and Thomas Babington Macaulay cannot fail to come away enriched.

We read the great books of American and English literature for their thoughts and truths, and we absorb from them the idioms and structure of our own language. But we should not stop there. The great books of other languages and other cultures are also part of our heritage. After we have absorbed our own literature and become grounded in our own culture, we should turn to world literature to hear, even in translation, the voices of other places and other times. For it is through books that we first learn of the infinite variety in life. Through books we can become the instant inhabitants of any time—past, present, or future— and any place.

We read not to remain passive but to liberate our minds for action. We become creative through our experience of books—as we permit Don Quixote, Hamlet, Ophelia, Captain Ahab, and Becky Sharp to excite our minds.

By means of books we learn, in a sense, to *become* others. As we read we identify with a character or a situation or a theme. C. S. Lewis, author of many imaginative novels of life on other planets, once expressed the wish that animals could write books, so that he would have been able to see things from the perspective of a mouse or a bee!

However far we can extend our sympathies through the

reading of fiction and nonfiction, classic and contemporary —to that degree we extend ourselves. This open-armed approach to reading must, of course, be mainly self-directed.

Reading provides for an expansion of the self. Reading widely and reading continuously does far more than just stock the mind with information or with models of expression. The crowding of many lives and experiences into our own can result in a remaking of the self. To some degree we are what we remember, and what we read is part of this. We write out of our stored-up knowledge and experience. Public occasions, historical events, the lives of others—all of these become means of expressing ourselves if they lodge in our memory.

The creative imagination will examine contemporary events, but it will do so in terms of an already established language and literature. Today will, as always, build on tradition. It is crippling to the creative impulse to read only books that describe the reader's own time and place. The immortal Ahab may have been captain of a nineteenth-century whaling ship, but the story of his obsession with Moby Dick has much to say to readers of today, and the *Pequod's* seahunt will stir living imaginations for many years to come.

The creative writer, it should be clear, grows through the cultivation of openness to new experiences and influences. "Be the kind of person upon whom nothing is lost," Henry James advises. "Observe, always observe." The range of your observation should include all the life you can get your hands on. Much of that life will be found, already captured, squirming, and vital, within the pages of books.

The ant in Aesop's fable, you may remember, was wiser than the grasshopper. The grasshopper frittered its time away, but the ant busied itself storing forage for a later day. Like the ant in the fable, the creative reader who is preparing to write will do well to take thought for the morrow. He or she will not be content solely to enjoy what others have written but will see reading as a source for use—to be imitated, added to, if possible improved upon, and, in every sense, enlarged.

Achievement, however, almost never comes quickly;

approval by others takes even longer. Learning to write and write well through the instrument of creative reading is often a process as lengthy as it is deliberate.

Readers on their way to becoming writers pay their predecessors the ultimate flattery, that of imitation. In its initial stages all art is imitative—whether it is painting, sculpture, the composition of music, or writing. The artist begins as imitator. Uniqueness and originality come later.

Robert Louis Stevenson, the essayist and novelist, described his own apprenticeship with great precision when he said that he "played the sedulous ape to Hazlitt." He started out sounding like the earlier essayist, but soon he was writing like himself and no one else.

Through a process of imitation and analysis you will accomplish two things. You will learn how to write, and you will learn more about yourself.

Experiment in imitating the style of others (imitating but not copying!). Cut, adapt, and strive to find the right word for *your* ideas on subjects others have written about before you. Train and shape your mind for clear thought and expression.

Such shaping cannot come about through the examination of the work of one's contemporaries alone. "A good style," F. Scott Fitzgerald once advised his daughter, "simply doesn't *form* unless you absorb a half dozen topflight authors every year." Familiarity with the acknowledged classics will enable you to more readily recognize today's top authors and to form a style that reflects the best of the past and the present.

Chapter 5.
It Could
Be Verse

"It is always a mistake," a literary critic once wrote, "not to be a poet." He meant this comment to apply to all writers— of prose as well as of verse. It is certainly true that if you, the prospective writer, avoid even reading poetry and lending eye and ear to what it is saying, you are depriving yourself of some of the richest resources of language.

One of the best and most efficient ways to become familiar with a language is to read and absorb its poetry. Poetry is the deep well from which words in their fullness of meaning may be drawn.

Any creative worker with words finds it necessary to make daily visits to the marketplace of language. Being alert to the rhythms of everyday speech and expression is being attentive to where words are alive. Words are alive in the dictionary as well, alive and waiting. Dig into your dictionary frequently, if only to browse. Check up on words you know; learn new words. Love words. A writer is one who is in love with words.

Poetry happens whenever thought and language collide. Poetry succeeds best when each word, each pause even (for the silences of verse are eloquent), seems freshly minted. Each word poetry uses is not merely a suitable word or an appropriate word. It is the *inevitable* word. Substitution is unthinkable; no other word will do.

Poetry's core is the naming of objects, as they exist both in the mind and outside of it. When Adam, according to Mark Twain, called the huge, furry object he encountered a "bear," Eve challenged him: "How do you know it's a bear?" she asked. Adam, the first poet, replied, "It looks like a bear."

The poet's first task is to say what things look like; the poet leaves their classification to the biologist or the philosopher. The poet, like Adam, goes around pointing at things with a finger of words. This is essential to the task of an essayist and of a novelist as well; they, too, name to depict.

One of the chief ways of naming, in poetry and in prose, is by comparing; another way is by contrasting. In poetry—where every word must count—we can see the definition of a subject grow, with meaning building upon meaning. Over and over and yet in a contained space, the poet is saying what *is.* An entity is defined not only by saying what it is, however. Meaning may be declared or clarified by the saying of what a thing is *not.* Much as a sculptor cuts away excess wood or marble to reveal the figure hidden within, the poet may proceed to define by paring away apparent likenesses.

Shakespeare's "Sonnet 18" demonstrates effectively what we may call definition by denial. Comparison of the subject's beauty is refused. Contrast succeeds contrast until the subject stands alone and is thus defined.

If you try to express the argument of this sonnet in prose, you will see that the poem's impact comes not so much from what it says as from those arrangements of contrast and rhyme the poet sets up to say it. Such "translations" from poetry to prose are worth doing for the discipline involved, especially if you are inclined, as many of us are, to slide over meaning when it comes to verse.

Trying to make prose of Shakespeare's verse, or, for that matter, of any verse, is legitimate and sensible, so long as you keep in mind that it is only creative in a "getting ready" sense—getting ready to create your own verse. Should Shakespeare seem too sacred to tamper with, select poems that have somewhat less of a literary reputation. It may be best to begin with a more primitive type, the ballad.

In the ballad the poet is storyteller. Ballads are a sort of middle ground between poetry and prose. They are neither epic nor lyric, yet they have elements of both. They are rhythmic short stories that often tell about ordinary people and ordinary events. Their origins are centuries old; they stem from a time when stories were told or sung, not written down. Rhyme helped the singer/storyteller to remember a tale long after the people and events that inspired it were forgotten. Style is a preservative, and these ballads, however unsophisticated their style, however crude their versifying, preserved the emotions and events of a past that would otherwise have been forgotten.

The study and imitation of the ballad can teach the young writer many things. Most of all, the ballad tells its story in a way that is both simple and subtle. Often the ballad jumps into the middle of its tale, leaving what went before to be guessed at. Ballads often switch from speaker to speaker with startling abruptness. You can learn from ballads what to leave out as well as what to put in. Read collections of ballads; Carl Sandburg's *The American Song-bag* (second edition, 1952) is an excellent place to start. Recordings of ballads by such contemporary artists as Burl Ives, Woody Guthrie, and Pete Seeger are also good sources.

After you have read and heard a number of ballads, try writing one about an event reported in your local newspaper. A highway accident, a tragic fire, a local gun battle— all these stories are prime ballad material. Or you might try a lyrical rather than a narrative ballad. Write about a love affair, plaintive or tragic, perhaps modeling it on the famous ballad about Barbara Allen, who dies for love, or on the story of Lord Randall, who was poisoned by his "true love."

Another source for ballad writing exercises is sheet music. Folk music, blue grass, rock, and other popular forms are already a kind of rough poetry. Sometimes they are highly stylized and sophisticated. Try rewriting a song by Bob Dylan, Mick Jagger, or the Beatles. "Sergeant Pepper's Lonely Hearts Club Band" is a lyric ballad, with a story line only lightly implied. Try rewriting it in rigid ballad form, switching speakers frequently and developing a more explicit story line.

Everything we have talked about thus far is for practice only and should be regarded as such. One should not mistake exercises, however helpful and formative, for the real thing. To do so would be rather like playing scales during a performance at Carnegie Hall.

After reading poetry for pleasure or for the purposes of imitation, what then? It may be that for many who undertake apprenticeship the results will be skill in doing the real thing. Out of constant experiment with form and feeling, a genuine competence with verse writing may emerge.

This emergence can be fostered by the practice of yet another form of poetry, one invented by the Japanese. In this form, known as the "haiku," the complete poem consists of seventeen syllables in three lines of verse: five/seven/five. The poem must have a single effect, presenting only one idea, feeling, or image.

To demonstrate the opportunities and challenges of the haiku, here is an early attempt at the form:

> A barren tree branch
> against a   sky
> makes a statement

This is a flawed beginning, to be sure. Three syllables are missing from the second line and one from the third. Here are two later attempts; the second is the final version, complete with title.

> A barren tree branch
> inhabited by a lone crow
> makes a statement.

(28)

PROTEST

The barren tree branch
harbors a visiting crow
to make a statement.

The next example is more complex. The poem went through more stages and is perhaps more successful.

SPARROWS FEEDING

Skydown they plummet
To conduct on docile feet
Polite inquiry.

This version achieves the correct number of syllables correctly placed, but there are at least two difficulties with it. Do sparrows really "plummet"? Hawks do, and Tennyson's eagle, but surely not sparrows. "To conduct" could easily be mistaken, at first glance, not for the intended infinitive but for a preposition and its noun object. (The poet must always be aware of grammar.) "Docile" is intended to contrast with "plummet," but does it do so?

The succeeding version removed these difficulties:

Skydown they tumble
To pursue on timid feet
Polite inquiry.

Further tinkering resulted in a new second line:

To pursue with timid steps

Now we turn to the final line. Is it too abstract? And just what does it mean?

A new attempt resulted in the substitution of two lines:

Skydown they tumble,
Then in excited whispering
Discuss the menu.

The second line went through several changes, none of them for the better. The final version reads as follows:

SPARROWS AT LUNCHTIME

Skydown they flutter,
Then to casual gossip
Discuss the menu.

The attempt has been—should always be—to make the word suit the action.

Writing haiku can be fun as well as instructive. Doing it successfully will give the writer confidence to attempt longer, more complicated forms, although writing haiku is a satisfaction in itself.

Ideas for haiku can be encountered anywhere and everywhere. Haiku may be suggested by the merest glimpses of the way nature—including human nature—reveals itself. Always keep pencil and paper on hand to capture haiku's elusive thought or word.

By means of haiku and other verse forms, from couplet to sonnet, one may learn to write in the only way it can be done—by writing.

Perhaps the next step after haiku would be to attempt another form based on syllable counting, the "cinquain." A relatively new form attributed to the American poet Adelaide Crapsey (1878–1914), the cinquain is a five-line poem with a syllabic structure: two/four/six/eight/two.

The cinquain looks simple to write, even easier than the haiku. Appearances, however, are deceptive, as the following attempts at composing a cinquain will demonstrate:

WEATHER REPORT

Storm cloud:
first paragraph
from beyond the mountains
of news that will settle down on
page one.

The initial version of "Weather Report" read:

> A cloud
> comes as byline
> for a news item, from
> beyond the next mountain, set in
> small type.

The difficulty with this version, which meets the syllable count requirement, seemed to lie in the use of the word "byline." The cloud is part of the story, not its author. And what is supposed to be in small type—the byline or the news item? (Another good question—why?)

The substitution of "dateline" for "byline" did not improve matters, nor did these versions of eight-syllable lines:

> with news that's fit to rewrite the
> with news ready to upset the
> of news confident of arriving on [nine syllables!]
> of news that will settle down on

Clearly, we can see that writing is a process of finding and arranging words, according to the demands of our thoughts and of the accepted form.

The next step in difficulty is to attempt the order imposed by rhyme. Rhyme provides the kind of exact discipline that the beginning writer needs and should welcome.

One of the attractive short rhymed forms is the triolet. This is a poem of eight lines. The first two lines reappear as the refrain of the two final lines; the first line also reappears in the middle of the poem as the fourth line. The rhyme scheme is as follows: A|B|a|A|A|b|A|B.

Here is an example of the triolet:

FORECAST

> A cold wind is blowing,
> and we shall have snow.
> The cattle are lowing.

(31)

A cold wind is blowing;
no grasses need mowing,
and water won't flow.
A cold wind is blowing,
and we shall have snow.

A more complicated rhymed form, and an even more intriguing and satisfying challenge, is the "villanelle," a medieval French form popular with modern poets. The villanelle requires an odd number of three-line stanzas (a, b, c) and a final four-line stanza. Here is an example of a villanelle.

WRITER'S CRAMP

I sing of pens and paper clips,
With baskets full of crumpled prose,
And coffee scorching tired lips.

My meals no more than fish and chips,
With hours snatched from my repose,
I sing of pens and paper clips.

I seek in vain for vivid quips,
With quests for rhyme among my woes,
And coffee scorching tired lips.

I'm haunted by rejection slips;
I've had by now my share of those.
I sing of pens and paper clips.

To reference books I make more trips.
I need ideas before I doze,
And coffee scorching tired lips.

My words come forth in sluggish drips.
I suffer from creation's throes.
I sing of pens and paper clips
And coffee scorching tired lips.

It should be noted that freedom in writing comes from following rules. The rules of verse form—fourteen for the sonnet, a measured five for the cinquain, etc.—offer challenges that nudge expression into being, that free the writer to look for, find, and express a subject in an individual and unique way. By means of experimenting with the various forms of prose and verse alike, one comes upon the secret to the art of writing. This secret, for most of us, turns out to be what Dylan Thomas calls the "sullen craft or art"—nothing more, nothing less than the stubborn and often stumbling effort of writing and rewriting.

Chapter 6.
Describing Life
with Sentences
that Move

"I never wanted two or three words in my life that I didn't know where to lay hands upon 'em," says Captain Cuttle in Dickens' *Dombey & Son.* "It comes of not wasting language as some do."

The pursuit of poetry teaches the creative writer not to "waste language" but to value each word, savor it, and put it to work. One learns from haiku, especially, to count every word and to make every word count. (This does not mean, of course, that one should set limits on one's word stock.)

Prose should be no more wasteful than verse; here too every word has its place and function. In prose as well as poetry, style counts. Of style, the scientist Thomas Henry Huxley wrote, "Say that which has to be said in such language that you can stand cross-examination on each word."

Good enough, but the problem remains: how do you find words when you need them?

For some people, words seem to appear effortlessly on paper; the writer is not able to put them down fast enough. For others the process of writing is a slow and agonizing one. Words simply will not come.

Yet both types, the swift and the slow, may be "born" writers—the latter a little more often than the former. Someone has defined writers as those for whom writing is more difficult than it is for other people.

Sculptors and writers seem to come in two kinds: those who cut away the excess and discover the work itself when the dust settles, and those who patiently build up layer after layer, much as nature builds a coral reef, one shell at a time.

The latter are known in the writing trade as "bleeders"; they "bleed" their words, drop by slow drop.

Of course the rate at which a creative person works, fast or slow, usually remains the artist's secret. False starts, strikeovers, and revisions—none of these show in a completed work. How long it takes a writer to arrive at a certain grouping of words should be as meaningless to the reader as the knowledge that a given passage was written on a Wednesday or a Thursday, or that the writer had a head cold the day it was done.

The worker in language starts with words; these are both the tools and the ingredients proper to the job. What words are appropriate for the task the writer assumes?

The ones that fit. Clearly these are not necessarily the first words that pop into the writer's mind. Words not to be used—to be examined and rejected—are those that occur to the writer not from direct observation or analysis but because they already hang on the rack, as ready for use as a threadbare sweater. Among such words are those defined as slang, discussed earlier, jargon, and vogue words— words on everybody's lips, words that can be used without much care or thought.

Sophistication in word choice comes from wide reading. The well-read reader/writer will be alert to the phrases that have been used over and over again or ones that are equally in danger of becoming hackneyed from overuse.

Take the platitudinous phrase, "the vicissitudes of life." It is some improvement to say, "the ups and downs of life." Unfortunately the improvement is slight. The result is still a cliché, an overused expression.

Reach out for words that come after a struggle, not ones that come neatly wrapped in a gift package. Reject the vague, general word, and search for the precise, specific one. Avoid long and unfamiliar words—"polysyllabics are to be eschewed"—in favor of those that are brief and direct.

Even the best choice of words is only the beginning, of course. Writing is the art of welding words together into sentences, paragraphs, and larger wholes.

The principle behind the art of joining words together—whether in verse, nonfiction, or fiction—is movement. A sentence is a unit that moves; it completes a journey—to use the terms of grammar—from subject to predicate. Thus in one sense the art of writing is the art of predicating sentences, leaping from subject to object by means of a verb.

Every sentence you write has a direction and a destiny; it is going *toward* something. All sentences and paragraphs start somewhere and end somewhere else.

To see how this works, assign yourself the task of writing sentences that move. Try describing physical movement first.

The man walked the length of the deserted alley. You have indicated physical movement here with the words "walked the length." You have also suggested a feeling with the adjective "deserted." You have even included an implied contradiction—itself a kind of mental movement: If the man is there, how can the alley be said to be deserted?

Now let's move into an extended use of movement:

> The man walked the length of the deserted alley. His movements were swift and furtive. Darting his eyes from side to side, he would pause now and then in a sagging doorway.

The expanded version adds editorial comment of course; it "moves" from description to commentary. The writer implies (but never quite says) something sinister about the person whose action was presented objectively in the first sentence. (Do not be afraid of an adjective or two here and there. "Sagging" can be justified as adding to the general sense of decay the writer is attempting to convey.)

A delicate balance is called for. If a word really "works," put it in. If it is inert or extra, take it out. Be careful not to "load" your prose in too relentless a pursuit of the lively, the unusual, or the unconventional in phrasing.

Often movement in a sentence is a movement in time. (Avoid the almost inevitable cliché here: "Time flew!")

> In five years the brothers had grown apart in their tastes. Charles, no longer the happy, outgoing young adventurer, had turned morose.

Here we have movement in time and in the effect of time.

The change wrought by time is also the topic of the paragraph that follows:

> Shall I tell you about the changes the last ten years have brought to my neighborhood? I can try. If you knew it from before, you will remember the old Haskins place —it was old, all right, and nobody in the Haskins family had lived there for over fifty years. It had been a boarding house, then an undertaker's parlor, and last of all, a short-lived boutique. Now it is gone, disappeared into a vast hole that took down half the block with it. Everything changes, they say, but does everything you grew up with, passed on the way to school or home from the movies (torn down now, for an office building) have to disappear?

Movement, in the mind and outside the mind, has consequences. It is almost impossible to mention a form of physical movement that does not imply, sometimes demand, other kinds of movement. The fun of dealing with facts is that they are potentially full of life. Facts need not lie cold and inert, either in the mind or on the page. They can "live" in relation to other facts; one fact tends to suggest another and another.

Tracing the relationship between facts or events and finding unexpected life or movement in the process is part of the pleasure we get (whether "bleeder" or not) from the constant practice of writing.

To show movement, it should be noted, is not necessarily to show motion. One can describe a scene that appears unmoving in space, yet it is moving—through time:

She sat at her desk while reading.

In the act of sitting, "she" occupies time as well as space, and time is always on the move.

Often, movement involves a continuing action, a chain of events:

As Peter slid down the steep bank, his hands grabbed wildly for a rock, a stump, a sapling—anything that would break the fall.

Peter's rapid journey was obviously a physical movement, set in time and space. It happened at a specific time; the bank was in a definite place. However this sentence contains still another kind of movement, a movement in thought and speculation. Three objects are mentioned that may or may not have actually been present—a rock, a stump, and a sapling. These words represent alternatives suggested to the mind—if not to Peter's, then at least to the mind of the person who composed the sentence. The reader is asked to sense the movement of a mind groping for possibilities of rescue in a dangerous situation—in addition to noting the purely physical movement.

Movement in logic may be found in the classic example of Patrick Henry's famous speech at the Virginia Convention, when he shouted among cries of treason, "Caesar had his Brutus! Charles I had his Cromwell!" then more mildly, "George III may profit by their example." The reader's mind moves with Patrick Henry's words and also outside of them. What is left unsaid is as clear as the words that were spoken.

For a contemporary example of movement throughout a single paragraph, examine the following from Paul Theroux's *The Old Patagonian Express,* an account of the author's journey by train to Argentina.

Every ten or fifteen minutes, the train halted. The soldiers jumped out and positioned themselves in a crouch on the ground, a firing position. Then a few people would hop to the ground and, without looking back at the train, begin walking into the desert—gone, lost behind the boulders—before the train started again. Most of these stations were not listed on the ticket; they were signboards, a clump of cactus, nothing more than that. Aguas Calientes was one of these: a sign, some cactus, a heap of rocks at the foot of a dry mountain. We started, and I saw a dry riverbed that mimicked a road, but near the riverbed an odd sight—great spurts of white steam from the hot springs that gave this place its name, bubbling from beneath that mountain which was a volcano. There were hot pools around the shooting steam, and women were doing their washing in them. Not even cactus could live among the geysers. The boiling water foamed in the bare rock and drained through the cracks; and the only live things visible in that dead corner of the desert were the bent-over women scrubbing their laundry.

Study the above for the movement—and the lack of movement—described in it. Use this paragraph as a model to create one of your own; choose as a subject either a place very familiar to you or a less familiar place you have observed and remembered. Aim for a contrast between motion and motionlessness.

In the excerpt above, many things are being seen; the point is that some*one* is in the act of seeing them, arranging them in memory perhaps, but definitely selecting and arranging them for a telling. Note how Theroux makes the paragraph "happen." First he gives us a general view of the train's frequent stops, with a vivid image of the soldiers (they are in Guatemala at this point) jumping out of the train at "stations not listed on the ticket." Then the train arrives at one of these stops, alike and yet different from the rest. The sterile terrain is described, and we are left with the image of the scrubwomen. What Theroux saw, of course, could have been seen by anyone. It was there to be seen. Whatever else there was to see that Theroux chose not to mention, we cannot know. This particular observer presents the facts in terms of what *he* saw—with his writer's eye excluding as well as including—and what he wants his *readers* to see.

In writing facts, you as the writer must do just this; you must be truthful, accurate, and fair. But you must also express truth as you understand it. Selection is part of writing and to some extent determines style. Anything you read, even if it is the most abstract, scientific textbook, will bear the author's personal touch, his or her style.

Behind everything written there is a person—someone who is seeing, interpreting, explaining, perhaps even enjoying. Fact remains fact, but it comes to us in a human way, spoken by an individual voice. Sometimes that voice even emanates from an opinionated, wrongheaded character like Captain Cuttle.

Through practice, you, too, can find your own voice in writing. You can put something of yourself in every sentence you place on paper.

Even if you write something as simple and seemingly unexciting as, "The horseman rode rapidly across the meadow," you have accomplished something. For one thing, you have avoided the excessive alliteration of "The rider rode rapidly across the road." And you have chosen your words wisely. They "fit"; they are precise, and they are accurate.

When you have acquired the skill of focusing with both clarity and purpose on the life around you as well as on the life within you, yours will be the delight, and the responsibility too, of the artist.

Chapter 7.
A World of Writing:
Letters, Journals,
News Stories and Such

There is a world of writing always at hand to be consulted for information and inspiration and to be imitated for the purposes of creative development.

All kinds of writing can help us see how writing is done, but perhaps the most useful to imitate, at least at first, is correspondence. Just as the born writer will ordinarily be a person given to continual reading, so he or she will also be one who feels a commitment to the use of words. And letters are a means of fulfilling that commitment.

In this electronic age, correspondence may slowly be becoming a lost art. Yet it continues to offer the creative writer a ready vehicle for communication with others and for self-exploration. A letter to a friend offers the opportunity to strike an attitude, to select a mood, and to filter thoughts and experiences through that mood. Correspondence, sent or unsent, offers the writer a choice of roles to act out.

The opportunity for social correspondence should never be neglected. It should, in fact, be cultivated. Through the artifice of letter writing, the art of writing itself becomes more natural.

By writing letters we not only explore and reveal our- selves (to ourselves and others), we also find and display our ideas.

Make it a habit to read the letters to the editor col- umns in your daily newspaper and in the magazines you read. There you will find people engaged in communication, perhaps commenting on events or on articles published in the newspaper or magazine, or perhaps rebutting a point of view expressed in an earlier letter to the editor.

Practice writing letters to an editor as a way of famil- iarizing yourself with your own "voice." If a letter turns out to be something more than an exercise in self-improvement, mail it in.

Read published correspondence from the past written by great political or literary figures. You will be exposing yourself to language perhaps more relaxed and flexible than that found in formal writing, yet still containing a purpose, either to inform, amuse, or motivate action. Two Americans in particular are worth your attention in this regard. Both wrote well and copiously; both had interesting minds and each worked very hard at writing letters. In their letters these two writers revealed themselves more fully and intimately than they did in their books—the mark of a great letter writer. The first, historian Henry Adams, was the descendant of two Presidents; the second, the late Flannery O'Connor, wrote numerous short stories.

Letter writing has another value for anyone wishing to use words and word structures creatively. The letter can be a vehicle not only for finding oneself, but for finding others as well. And one can put those found down on paper, in fiction.

To see a particularly effective use of letter writing *within* a novel, turn to the pages of Jane Austen's *Pride and Prejudice*. The letters the great comic character Mr. Collins writes certainly help to establish his personality for the reader and for the other characters in the novel. Mr. Col- lins enters the story in Chapter 13, by means of a letter so pompous and absurd that the heroine, Elizabeth Bennet, after hearing it read aloud asks her father, "Can he be a sensible man, sir?" Mr. Collins is clearly not a sensible man, as his subsequent letters and actions toward Elizabeth show. But his character is first glimpsed in the letter that announces his presence in the novel.

Another way to develop skill in the writing of prose is to keep a diary or journal. Here the effort can remain private, for the writer's eyes only, unless—as often happens —the writer later chooses to use some of the entries elsewhere.

Following is an entry from the notebooks of Paul Horgan, a novelist and historian of the American Southwest.

> I saw her merely turn her head, in the throng, at a party;
> and I knew her whole life—for my purposes, that is, as
> a novelist.

Horgan's claim, breathtakingly expressed, is often true of the literary artist. Just a glimpse can reveal a world for the writer of fiction.

In another notebook entry, Horgan observes, in meticulous detail, an action that seems to say something about character. The first sentence is not really a sentence. It is the initial observation that drew the writer into a careful witnessing of the events that followed.

> The man paralyzed from the waist down being wheeled on a winter afternoon in a small neat compact chromium wheelchair to his Rolls Royce limousine parked at the curb in 54th Street. On his lap is balanced an attaché case. There is a young woman waiting at the car—a nurse?—in a winter overcoat. The man wheeling him turns him to the open front door of the car. The nurse takes away the left armrest of the chair and attempts to remove the attaché case. He slaps her away from it. With his right hand and arm he arranges his inert legs to a slanting position for moving. She sets a smooth board from the car's front seat to the raised footrest of the wheelchair. He turns himself to sit on the board. He then hunches and grubs himself along into the car. His

movements are like those of a seal out of water. Finally he is in, the board is removed, the chair is folded and stowed in the rear of the car, the attendants get into the car, she driving, and all doors are shut. During the maneuver the slim, shiny, black attaché case has remained on his lap, and as they drive away, he clutches it to his breast.

Notice carefully what happens here. The author is describing a sequence of actions, with every detail accounted for—the left armrest, the man's right hand and arm, etc. Why, one may ask, the adjective "winter" for overcoat? Is the heavy coat somehow inappropriate for the day? Would Horgan clarify this point if the passage were to be lifted from the notebook and put into a story? Note the unusual verb "grubs." Webster's dictionary defines this word "to do menial work; to plod; drudge." Is it well chosen here? Is it deliberately insensitive to or critical of the paralyzed man? If so, why?

Both of the passages quoted from Horgan's notebooks can serve as models for the apprentice. The first presupposes mature judgment perhaps, but that is any writer's objective, however far off at the moment. The second suggests that even everyday occurrences should be captured in words. In addition, it shows what can be done with sustained observation.

When the writer looks up from the daily journal, he or she should then turn to the daily newspaper. The newspaper is a link to the freshly written word. It communicates to us in the form of news stories, of course, and news stories are excellent sources of information and of things to write about. The newspaper also provides models for writing—through editorials, by-lined columns, sports features, and articles on homemaking and entertainment.

A feature story is "soft" news, as compared to the "hard" news item that reports what has just happened, what is new, significant, and startling. The feature article is less timely than the news item but also more timeless. It rewards human curiosity. For American newspaper readers, feature stories about children and animals rank high in popularity. There also seems to be great interest in free flight—in parachutists, eagles, balloons, and so on. The first day in spring that the bears use their outdoor pool is always worth at least a photograph and a caption. (A suggested assignment: write a feature story suggested by a newspaper photograph.) Other stories that serve to counterbalance the day's ration of grim events might be the reunion of a brother and sister separated for half a century or the story of a local Irish Sweepstakes winner. These carry strong reader identification. Human interest stories are feature stories focusing on people. Feature stories may also focus on problems or issues.

Newspapers provide a steady flow of feature articles that can serve as models of content and style. So do magazines, including mass circulation publications such as *TV Guide* and *Reader's Digest* as well as the more literary types such as *Harper's* and the *Atlantic.* Week after week the "Talk of the Town" section of the *New Yorker* contains short human interest and feature articles of outstanding quality.

It might prove a useful exercise to rewrite a feature article found in the *New Yorker* or elsewhere. Use the piece as your source of facts. Then for contrast, find a feature story in a more science-oriented journal. Avoid a highly technical magazine; instead, choose one intended to make science understandable to the layperson. When you locate an appropriate article, compare it to your feature story. Note the difference in language. Is it more formal because it is about science? It may not be. Casual language is often used in these articles to lighten a dry or technical subject. Note also the method of research employed. In many feature stories a personal interview is used. Library research is the chief source of information for other feature stories. Using different leads, try rewriting the article from the science journal.

Newspapers and magazines will keep you up to date on issues and events. They can help provide valuable literary information and form literary taste. The reading of book reviews and literary articles in these sources can help develop skill in judging literary quality, even the quality of your own writing.

Finally, to free yourself from too much reliance upon models, you might try writing from facts, perhaps using as a reference a book of lists. The list you choose can furnish your content; what you do with it will be a result of your style and approach.

Chapter 8.
A Fling at
Fiction

Up came the sun, streaming all over London, and in its glorious impartiality even condescending to make prismatic sparkles in the whiskers of Mr. Alfred Lammle as he sat at breakfast. In need of some brightening from without was Mr. Alfred Lammle, for he had the air of being dull enough within, and looked grievously discontented.

Mrs. Alfred Lammle faced her lord. The happy pair of swindlers, with the comfortable tie between them that each had swindled the other, sat moodily observant of the tablecloth. Things looked so gloomy in the breakfast-room, albeit on the sunny side of Sackville Street, that any of the family tradespeople glancing through the blinds might have taken the hint to send in his account and press for it. But this, indeed, most of the family tradespeople had already done, without the hint.

"It seems to me," said Mrs. Lammle, "that you have had no money at all ever since we have been married."

"What seems to you," said Mr. Lammle, "to have been the case, may possibly have been the case. It doesn't matter."

Was it the speciality of Mr. and Mrs. Lammle, or does it ever obtain with other loving couples? In these matrimonial dialogues they never addressed each other, but always some invisible presence that appeared to take a station about midway between them. Perhaps the skeleton in the cupboard comes out to be talked to, on such domestic occasions?

"I have never seen any money in the house," said Mrs. Lammle to the skeleton, "except my own annuity. That I swear."

"You needn't take the trouble of swearing," said Mr. Lammle to the skeleton; "once more, it doesn't matter. You never turned your annuity to so good an account."

"Good an account! In what way?" asked Mrs. Lammle.

"In the way of getting credit, and living well," said Mr. Lammle.

Perhaps the skeleton laughed scornfully on being intrusted with this question and this answer; certainly Mrs. Lammle did, and Mr. Lammle did.

"And what is to happen next?" asked Mrs. Lammle of the skeleton.

"Smash is to happen next," said Mr. Lammle to the same authority.

After this, Mrs. Lammle looked disdainfully at the skeleton—but without carrying the look on to Mr. Lammle—and drooped her eyes. After that, Mr. Lammle did exactly the same thing, and drooped *his* eyes. A servant then entering with toast, the skeleton retired into the closet, and shut itself up.

"Sophronia," said Mr. Lammle, when the servant had withdrawn. And then, very much louder: "Sophronia!"

"Well?"

"Attend to me, if you please." He eyed her sternly until she did attend, and then went on. "I want to take counsel with you. Come, come; no more trifling. You know our league and covenant. We are to work together for our joint interest, and you are as knowing a hand as I am. We shouldn't be together if you were not. What's to be done? We are hemmed into a corner. What shall we do?"

"Have you no scheme on foot that will bring in anything?"

Mr. Lammle plunged into his whiskers for reflection, and came out hopeless: "No; as adventurers we are obliged to play rash games for chances of high winnings, and there has been a run of luck against us."

What is happening here?

When we read this passage, which is from the opening of a chapter in Charles Dickens' *Our Mutual Friend,* several things are happening—to us and in us.

First of all, Mr. and Mrs. Alfred Lammle, who have never existed, come to life in our minds as we read.

What confers existence upon them? The creativity of Dickens in thinking them up and then our receptivity, our conspiratorial consent almost, to accept in our imaginations everything the author tells us.

What makes the excerpt we just read believable? Not the mere mention of London or the sun. What Mr. and Mrs. Lammle do and what they say—what an unidentified narrator tells us about what they do and say—speaks to us with much the same authority as a historian might in writing of the Tower of London.

We accept the Lammles as existing because what they say to one another seems real to us. Financial difficulties are universal, not confined to a particular city or period. The financial difficulties of the Lammles are universal, yet particular to them.

The couple exist in another way. They enter our minds not only because of what they do and say but also because of the manner, the tone, in which they are presented to us.

We are aware of this tone almost at once. The sun in this passage is a very special sun indeed. It shines even upon Alfred Lammle, giving a sparkle to his whiskers. We are aware almost at once that a very partial attitude toward the Lammles is being offered to us.

The second paragraph makes this attitude even clearer. The Lammles, we are told, are a "happy pair of swindlers."

In the first two paragraphs we are told about this happy pair. The narrator's voice presents them to us. With the third paragraph, the action begins. Mrs. Lammle speaks, and then her husband. First it was *tell,* and now it is *show.* The Lammles come alive.

Although the dialogue between the two is far from brilliant, it does give a sense of realism. It goes from one point to another. It is not idle. It accumulates meaning.

It is also worth noting how Dickens uses the dialogue here to lead us in a particular direction without our being aware of it. What is that direction? We go from the narrator telling the story to the Lammles taking it over and telling it themselves, for a time, anyway. This device must be subtle to be effective. Otherwise the reader would be aware of the shift and the sense of realism would be damaged.

The Lammles take over the story for a time, but even during this time there is still another storyteller present. This is the narrator, the one who provides us with the comic notion of "the skeleton" they both address rather than each other.

Although this is but a slight episode in a long chapter, and the chapter is in a very long book, the passage quoted has a certain wholeness of its own. The narrator rounds the incident out, takes the story back from the Lammles, as it were, with the second reference to Mr. Lammle's whiskers. The sun made sparkles in them earlier; now Mr. Lammle "plunges" into them to think.

Fiction is story—people saying things, people doing things. These sayings and doings can be made to seem real through descriptive techniques that enable us to see the characters in a setting. But no matter how real the story seems—even if actual historical figures and events are described—the result is not ordinary reality but a special kind of reality. The actual has been reconstructed, recreated by the writer's imagination.

This reconstruction—of bits and pieces of what actually exists and bits and pieces of what has been imagined— must be believable.

Credibility is a goal of the nonfiction writer too, but it might be said to be especially the goal of the writer of fiction. Fiction, after all, is basically *as if.* But it must give the impression of *as is.*

Suppose Dickens had written: "Up came the sun, streaming all over London, the capital of France, a steaming tropical city. . . ."

Everything is lost. No matter how engagingly Dickens presented the Lammles after that, we would not pay attention. We could not be made to care. Fiction is a make-believe world that must bring in the real world in an accurate but selective way. Fiction is based on fact. It extends it; it must not fracture it.

The writing of fiction presents a unique opportunity for the writer to extend the self, to become another self for a while.

As the writer of nonfiction you remain yourself. Through quotation and anecdote in nonfiction, you *represent* the thoughts and opinions and life experiences of others. You do not *become* these others. We read and write nonfiction to understand. But we read and write fiction to empathize and to become.

In fiction, both as reader and writer you are given a chance to think the thoughts and have the experiences of a second life. You imagine that life as you write fiction, selecting the exchanges of dialogue and interaction that will make such a life real in your own mind. What you create in fiction is a contained universe.

It may occur to you that since fiction is imagined, made up, reading fiction is a waste of time, useful only to escape for a brief time the difficulties of reality. After all, the people in fiction aren't real people; what they say or do doesn't really affect anything, at least in the real world. Just what is the point in reading it then, or trying to write it?

It is true that you can be a creative person without reading or writing fiction. But you are missing out on some of the greatest satisfactions that can come to anyone.

"What is a novel?" Jane Austen asks in an unaccustomed outburst in her novel *Northanger Abbey.* "Only," she answers herself, "some work in which the greatest powers of the mind are displayed, in which the most thorough knowledge of human nature, the happiest delineation of its varieties, the liveliest effusions of wit and humor are conveyed to the world in the best chosen language."

No doubt she exaggerates a little, but she makes an important point: fiction teaches us much of what we know about human nature and life.

Fiction also lives in a way that fact does not. Examples are plentiful, but one may suffice. Henry James once wrote a short story entitled "The Last of the Valerii." James's biographer, Leon Edel, tells us that this story was based upon the author's reaction to certain newspaper reports of events during a noteworthy period in Rome.

Newspaper stories of that period are now forgotten, but the Rome of that time is still alive. It is alive through the fiction that James wrote about it. It springs to new life every time a person picks up the story and reads it.

Or take an example from fictionalized history. Shakespeare's plays, everyone agrees, are alive and fresh. They continue to be read by millions. Now, through television, they are being viewed by many millions more.

When Shakespeare was writing his plays and they were first being performed, Queen Elizabeth I was alive and seated on the British throne. What of her now? Lady Macbeth, Calpurnia, Rosalind, and Desdemona are all more alive than she. Through historical scholarship, Elizabeth can be presented and re-presented. She can be portrayed in biography or even made the protagonist of a novel. But her mind cannot be known in the way and to the extent that Shakespeare's mind can be known. Her thoughts, unlike his, no longer live. Elizabeth was; Juliet—and thus Shakespeare —is.

Literature lives in a fuller and more intense way than history. And fiction, for our time, is the form of literature that most fully receives and confers life.

For all the differences between them, and in spite of the fact that fiction's people, places, and events are imagined rather than real, fiction and nonfiction have much in common. Both exist in time and space. Like fact, fiction has a beginning, a middle, and an end. The path through fiction therefore resembles the path through fact; it takes movement to go from one stage to another in both.

We call the main stages of movement in fiction *complication, climax,* and *resolution.* They usually occur in that order. Most often complication occupies the greatest amount of printed space. Climax ordinarily comes near the end; resolution is the end. Put less technically, peoples' lives become snarled and entangled in a problem; the solution of these difficulties leads to new problems, to be solved in turn. When the leading character has no more options, when things can go only one way, we are at the climax. The resolution offers the final solution, the wrap-up. Taken together, the stages of this physical and psychological journey can be called the story line, or plot.

Fiction resembles nonfiction in that it can be narrated as a first-person experience (I) or as an objective, third-person (he, she) account. Our language is rich in fiction presented in both persons, perhaps more often in the latter than in the former. (For short stories written in the first person, read those of Poe; Henry James offers tales told from both the first and third angles of narration. For a novel in the first person and all that the use of that angle implies, read Mark Twain's *Huckleberry Finn;* for third-person narrative, read *Tom Sawyer.*)

In fiction there is a narrative device that combines the advantages of both the first- and third-person angles of narration. This is the viewpoint character, a character whose mind the reader enters and whose thoughts are given as that person's thoughts. This device enables the reader to know a character both from the inside, the way we know ourselves, and from the outside, the way we know others. The effect is that the reader is drawn into the story more fully and becomes more caught up in the events because he or she has greater empathy for one of the characters. The advantages for the writer here are equally great. The viewpoint character allows the writer to *become* someone else by entering the mind of another. This is something that fiction can do with a conviction and credibility possible to no other form.

See for yourself how this can work. Did your father ever tell you about an incident from his boyhood? Has a neighbor revealed an experience he or she had years ago in another country? Try turning any facts you can gather into fiction by *becoming* these others, by making them viewpoint characters whose minds you possess. "The man thought. . . ." (But you were never inside your father's mind.) "She looked at him for a long moment and wondered." (You *imagine* what your neighbor wondered.)

Fiction can be fun to write; it can be a means of self-knowledge, a release from tension, and a way to discover what others do and why they do it.

For your first fling at fiction, you might like to try writing variations of the passage from Dickens with which this chapter begins. Here are some of the ways that will enable you to enjoy the satisfactions (and experience the problems) of being imaginative and creative:

1. Retell the passage with Mr. Lammle as a first-person narrator. (He might have the idea that he alone addresses the "skeleton." On the other hand, see what happens if he thinks that only Mrs. Lammle does it.)

2. Retell the passage with Mrs. Lammle as a viewpoint character—enter her mind only, not Mr. Lammle's.

3. Change the tone. Instead of Dickens' light banter, use a grim tone. The subject certainly has somber possibilities.

4. Describe the characters physically; let us know, from the third-person narrator's point of view, what each looks like. Elsewhere in *Our Mutual Friend,* Dickens, in a mixture of summary and description, characterizes Alfred Lammle as follows: "A mature young gentleman with too much nose on his face . . . too much sparkle in his studs, his eyes, his buttons, his talk and his teeth." Decide upon a face and appearance for Mrs. Lammle.

5. Make a complete story from the excerpt given by supplying a plot that either reconciles the two and solves their financial problems or perhaps one that completes their financial ruin and separates them.

6. Turn the episode into a contemporary story, using as the setting a place or city you know well.

Chapter 9.
How a Writer
Works

Observe a child at play in a sandbox. Note the elaborate care and seriousness with which the child is patting the sand, pushing it, or scooping it up. See how wrinkled the child's brow is from the effort of concentration. Beads of perspiration may even be forming on the child's forehead.

What is the child doing?

The obvious answer, of course, is that the child is playing. Yet note the signs of struggle, the unrelenting determination to impose a pattern, to make a design, in the sand. The child is working.

Actually, the child is not really either working or playing. The child is doing something that combines both: the child is creating.

In the creative act, work and play are brought together. The act is work: energy is being used and matter displaced. Yet the child performs with pleasure. The child is experiencing some measure of the rapture of the artist.

For the artist, for the writer, working is playing—playing with words. The writer comes equipped with the tools of grammar and rhetoric. The writer's game is to pat words and push them around, discover patterns, and arrive at meaning.

The process for the writer, and for the child in the sandbox, combines work and play: work in a playful manner, play that is worklike. As Tom Sawyer discovered, not being obliged to work makes working playful; being obliged to do it well, once involved, makes it work.

In the process of play the writer becomes very serious. The purpose of all play is to accomplish something, to make something that did not exist before. The writer works in the spirit of play—dreaming, doing, observing. Words, as we know, have a kind of life of their own. When they meet and merge in new combinations what they form and celebrate is new life. To participate in this is to play.

Poets play, and their play becomes poems.

Essayists and short story writers, playwrights, and novelists—though their games may take longer—also engage in the playful exploration of words.

One way of learning how to write would be to watch professionals in action. This is not very practical, however. Another way is to see the work of great authors in various stages of development. Only a very few authors have allowed us this privilege. One who did was Nathaniel Hawthorne.

Although Hawthorne is best remembered today for his grim novel of Puritan life in New England, *The Scarlet Letter,* he had his first success with a much lighter work, a retelling of classic Greek stories called *Wonder Book.* The words Hawthorne uses to describe the fictional narrator of that book, Cousin Eustace, apply to almost any successful author. Cousin Eustace was, says Hawthorne, "as fond of telling his stories as the children of hearing them. His mind was in a free and happy state, and took delight in its own activity, and scarcely required any external impulse to set it to work." Hawthorne appropriately calls Cousin Eustace's outlook "the spontaneous play of the intellect."

Hawthorne left us a large body of private work, collected under the titles *American Notebooks, English Notebooks,* and the *French* and *Italian Notebooks.* They contain three types of notations: diary entries obviously intended to provide material for later rewriting; complete essays ready to be sent out to editors; and "germ" ideas of stories and sketches. In these pages we see a writer busy in his workshop, constantly engaged in work and play, and struggling to find the right format for his ideas.

Many of Hawthorne's notebook entries record what he saw on his daily walks. Here is an example:

> In my walk yesterday forenoon I passed an old house which seemed to be quite deserted. It was a two-story, wooden house, dark and weather-beaten. The front windows, some of them, were shattered and open, and others were boarded up. Trees and shrubbery were growing neglected, so as quite to block up the lower part. There was an aged barn near at hand, so ruinous that it had been necessary to prop it up. There were two old carts, both of which had lost a wheel. Everything was in keeping. At first I suspected that there would be no inhabitants in such a dilapidated place; but, passing on, I looked back, and saw a decrepit and infirm old man at the angle of the house, its fit occupant. The grass, however, was very green and beautiful around this dwelling, and, the sunshine falling brightly on it, the whole effect was cheerful and pleasant. It seemed as if the world was so glad that this desolate old place, where there was never to be any more hope and happiness, could not at all lessen the general effect of joy.

In the above Hawthorne does two things: he describes what he saw, and, in the final sentence particularly, he strikes an attitude about it. Simple observation, however, rather than a deep probing for significances is all that Hawthorne is attempting here.

Later Hawthorne published a sketch entitled "The Old Apple Dealer." In this sketch he describes an old man, not as the man might casually be encountered in life, but as he might be "posed" for the reader, or, in Hawthorne's words, "represented to the imaginative vision by word painting." This particular word portrait is more than an attempt to pin on paper—as a photograph might—a subject seen just once and then only briefly. This portrait is the result of long, conscious, and, as Hawthorne is at pains to point out, subconscious study. "I have," Hawthorne writes, "studied the old apple dealer until he has become a naturalized citizen of my inner world."

Here is a workshop secret indeed. We are reminded that the writer should not only see the externals of what is being written about, but that the object observed actually should become part of one's inner world—literally of one's insight.

In the following paragraph from "The Old Apple Dealer" we can see Hawthorne at work (and at verbal play) as he makes clear to himself and to us the "vision" of his portrait:

He is a small man, with gray hair and gray stubble beard, and is invariably clad in a shabby surtout of snuff color, closely buttoned, and half concealing a pair of gray pantaloons; the whole dress, though clean and entire, being evidently flimsy with much wear. His face, thin, withered, furrowed, and with features which even age has failed to render impressive, has a frost-bitten aspect. It is a moral frost which no physical warmth or comfortableness could counteract. The summer sunshine may fling its white heat upon him, or the good fire of the depot room may make him the focus of its blaze on a winter's day; but all in vain; for still the old man looks as if he were in a frosty atmosphere, with scarcely warmth enough to keep life in the region about his heart. It is a patient, long suffering, quiet, hopeless, shivering aspect. He is not desperate,—that, though its etymology implies no more, would be too positive an expression,—but utterly devoid of hope. As all his past life, probably, offers no spots of brightness to his memory, so he takes his present poverty and discomfort as entirely a matter of course: he thinks it the definition of existence, so far as himself is concerned, to be poor, cold, and uncomfortable. It may be added that time has not thrown dignity as a mantle over the old man's figure: there is nothing venerable about him: you pity him without scruple.

When this paragraph is compared to the earlier one, the reader sees at once that the second is far more complex. Hawthorne is in this excerpt attempting to "see" on at least two levels. He accounts for surfaces, and then he interprets what the eye cannot see but the mind has come to understand. As the entire sketch reveals, the apple dealer has indeed entered Hawthorne's mind and taken up citizenship there.

Another notebook entry of Hawthorne's was a "germ" idea later used in a "moralized legend" entitled "Feathertop": "To make a story out of a scarecrow, giving it odd attributes. From different points of view, it should appear to change,—now an old man, now an old woman,—a gunner, a farmer, or Old Nick."

It might be fun to try to write such a story, perhaps giving it a Halloween motif. Choose one of the "points of view" Hawthorne suggested and write your sketch before turning to see what Hawthorne did with it.

Hawthorne has done even more than leave notebook entries that reveal his craft to the beginning writer. In his unfinished short story "Wakefield," he has given us an extended view of himself busy at play in his workshop.

"Wakefield" is the story of a man who leaves home on a business trip and stays away for twenty years. "Something of this kind actually happened in London," Edgar Allan Poe tells us in his review of Hawthorne's *Twice-Told Tales,* where the story appears. "The force in Mr. Hawthorne's tale," Poe writes in his book review, "lies in the analysis of the motives which must or might have impelled the husband to such folly, in the first instance, with the possible causes of his perseverance. Upon this thesis a sketch of singular power has been constructed."

In "Wakefield" Hawthorne deliberately leaves parts of the story vague, even suggesting that the reader help him to write the story. "What sort of man was Wakefield?" he asks the reader. "We are free to shape out our own idea, and call it by his name." (Here is a hint to try writing your own version of the story.)

In this story, Hawthorne seems to be abdicating the fiction writer's responsibility entirely. He sets up a situation, brings the reader to a high point of expectation and suspense, and then backs away. No writer should tantalize and deprive the reader this way. But that is Hawthorne's point, of course. He is not really telling us a story in the usual way; he is showing us the possibilities of fiction.

Afterword

What would you say if someone asked your opinion about the practical use of learning to write creatively?

Benjamin Franklin, when asked a similar question, replied, "What use is a baby?"

Many creative writers are content to experiment with words for their own private satisfaction. They use the activity as a way to release tensions, as an opportunity to get to know themselves better, and as a means of expanding themselves.

Others may not wish to leave it at that. Unless and until these writers see themselves in print, they will remain dissatisfied. Those who see publication as a long-term goal, to be achieved only after considerable practice, stand a chance for professional success.

But what about those who simply want to improve their writing skills? Is creative writing a waste of time for them? And how about those writers who try but never achieve publication? Are they gaining anything worthwhile for their efforts?

One goal of this book has been to show that creative writing is worthwhile for any purpose. To possess the ability to think with precision and to express one's thoughts clearly is to have great personal power. And creative writing can give you this power.

It is always a mistake to be in exile from language, to be a hostage to gobbledegook or doublethink. To use the language of others and not your own is to walk around in someone else's clothes.

More than that, freedom and democracy ultimately depend upon citizens who are capable of knowing when language is being used to inform honestly and when it is being used to dishonestly conceal.

Especially in this age of mass communication, when it is so easy to allow the media—television, newspapers, press releases, etc.—to do your thinking for you, you have an obligation, to yourself and to others, to be a creative person.

Being a creative person means, as we have been saying, being in touch with your uniqueness and sharing that uniqueness with others. Through your efforts to write creatively, through your attempts to become familiar with words and stay attuned to living language, you can become that creative person.

Index